PRAISE FOR *LIKE BUDDHA-CALM BIRD*

Kevin Rabas's new collection of poems and stories *Like Buddha-Calm Bird*, improvises on and riffs off the variable rhythms of the stories we create, revise, and live. Writing the music inherent in changing narratives of the ordinary and extraordinary. Rabas illustrates what a fellow Kansas poet meant when he said, "Anyone who breathes is in the rhythm business, anyone who is alive is caught up in the imminences, the doubts mixed with the triumphant certainty, of poetry." Whether writing about Ugandan rain, the Bossa Nova, a middle school drummer, or the T. Rex at a museum, Rabas puts his ear to what wants to be said, then moseys into words slow and deliberate, or explodes into language fast and on the wing. In a sense, much of this collection leads up the final section, "Eclipse," showing us how we partner with the life force to co-create this world: "the breath of God/ comes in a cloud" and "an open/mouth whistles/ over and past tall grasses/ from dust, remakes the world."

> Caryn Mirriam-Goldberg, Kansas Poet Laureate 2009-13, and author of *Everyday Magic: Fieldnotes on the Mundane and Miraculous*

Like Buddha-Calm Bird, by Kansas Poet Laureate, Kevin Rabas, is a gift of captured moments offered to his many readers and admirers. The intrepid poet never blinks, never misses a detail, wielding his pen as a surgeon does a scalpel, dissecting the butterfly without blemishing its beauty. Intimacy during a speakeasy gig, embarrassment at a jazz drummers' clinic, humor in an exercise class, humiliation from a bully, and tenderness with his soulmate are among the moments pondered and presented in Rabas's fearless voice. As always, his words ring true.

> Michael D. Graves, author of *To Leave a Shadow* and *Shadow of Death*

Like Buddha-Calm Bird
Copyright © 2018 Kevin Rabas

Meadowlark (an imprint of Chasing Tigers Press)
P.O. Box 333
Emporia, Kansas 66801
meadowlark-books.com

Kevin Rabas
PO Box 274
Emporia, KS 66801
krabas3@yahoo.com or krabas@emporia.edu
kevinrabas.com

Cover photos: "Like Buddha-Calm Bird" by Dave Leiker
daveleikerphotography.com

Cover design: Eric Sonnakolb

Cover sculpture: "Charlie Parker Memorial," by Robert Graham
Note the sculpture depicted on the front cover of this book is the "Charlie Parker Memorial" sculpture, © 2018 Robert Graham Studio / Artists Rights Society (ARS), New York. Image used with permission.

"Cardenio Modern" font (used on cover, titles, and page numbers and headers throughout this book) by Nils Cordes, nilscordes.com - licensed under the Creative Commons Attribution-ShareAlike 4.0 International License

All rights reserved. This book or any portion thereof
may not be reproduced or used in any manner whatsoever
without the express written permission of the author
except for the use of brief quotations in a book review.

ISBN: 978-1-7322410-2-2

Library of Congress Control Number: 2018951387

LIKE BUDDHA-CALM BIRD
BY KEVIN RABAS

A MEADOWLARK BOOK

ALSO BY KEVIN RABAS:

POETRY

Bird's Horn & Other Poems
Lisa's Flying Electric Piano
Sonny Kenner's Red Guitar
Eliot's Violin
Songs for My Father
All That Jazz
Late for Cymbal Line

FICTION

Spider Face: stories
Green Bike: a group novel
(with Mike Graves and Tracy Million Simmons)

"Charlie Parker looked like Buddha . . . and his expression on his face was as calm, beautiful, and profound as the image of the Buddha . . . the lidded eyes, the expression that says, 'All is well.'"

Jack Kerouac

for Lisa Moritz,
Dennis Etzel Jr, Doug Talley, Roy Gunter, Sharon Eiker,
and Chuck Haddix

LIKE BUDDHA-CALM BIRD
CONTENTS

1. NARRATIVES

Not Done 3
Ugandan Rain, Banana Leaf 4
In Rubonis, Uganda, in the Rwenzori Mountains:
Service Learning 5
Orchestra Concert Walk 6
Flag Scoop 7
Snatching Rip's Hi-Hat 9
Speakeasy Gig, or Playing for Me 11

2. (MORE) NEW MUSIC OR BOSSA NOVA, THAT NEW NEW THING

Dennis Chambers, Recorded 15
Bossa Nova, That New New Thing 16
Blues Guitar 17
How James Keller Lost His Groove 18
One Week Off 19
Mix'n' 20
"Seven Days" 21
Weekend Gig 22

Commencement Processional:
"Triumphant March" from "Aida" 23
New Tune, Juan's Song 24
New Tune 25
Middle School Drummer 26

3. ELECTION DAY

The Donald 29
[Hillary's Sunk] 30
Golden Shower 31
Patsy 32
We Read (#2) 33
Election Day Map 34

4. MEN AND WOMEN

Change Drawer Lip Balm 37
Good Form 38
Eclipse 39
Pit Stop 40
Out Again 41
Because I'm Already Involved 42
We See What We Want 43
Pear Shaped 44

5. KIDS

HiFi 47
T. Rex, Sternberg Museum, Hays, KS 48
Day Off 49
The Fourth 50
Afterburner at the Up-Down Retro Video Game Café 51
Cute Li'l Groot 52
Neighborhood Hood 53

6. DOCUMENTARY SHOTS

Wedding Shots 57
Your Portrait 58
Photos in the Field 59
Saving 60
Water Break 61
Fuzzy's 62
Don't Look 63
Lisa Redoes the Room 64

7. ECLIPSE

Eclipse, Emporia, Kansas 67
Transitory 68
Cottonwood 69
The slow turn 70
Roadtrip, Rainbow 71
White Hair 72
Write Right Like Buddha-Calm CP 73
Weed Whip Line, Caught 74
Friday, 5 O'Clock 75
Strings 76
Line 77
Brown Suede Sports Coat 78
Wait in the Lot 79
Poet 80

About the Author 81
Primary Current Influences 81
Acknowledgments 83
Words of Thanks 85

I. NARRATIVES

Not Done
        with Gary Wyatt

We eat tilapia
by the sea, that little
black fish with a small pinch
of salt to season the dish
in Uganda, where this
is a lot, a treat, more than most
ever eat, and we stop,
and the waiter says, "Not done,"
so we pick the bones.
"Not done." So we eat
the scales, fins. "Not done."
So we eat the eyes, warm
and soft, the tail
'til there is nothing
left but thin
white bones, like hooks,
like teeth, like the belly
of a boat, stripped, open
to the sun and sea,
hollow, a mouth
all the way open, hungry
for nothing now.

Ugandan Rain, Banana Leaf
with Gary and Ranae Wyatt

I go to the Seussical cell phone tree
and leave my second message
that week, "Hi, I'm fine. Tell
your other brothers," and, phone in hand,
I forget the clouds, sun gone under,
coming rain, and the drops
fall like little little rocks, like pebbles,
stones, and I'm left
without cover, and a teen
sees me, jogs to the forest
and cuts a big banana leaf
with his machete, gives me
shelter, like an open boat,
that banana leaf above
my crown. He does not
cut one for himself.

In Rubonis, Uganda, in the Rwenzori Mountains: Service Learning
with Gary and Ranae Wyatt

End of the day
   of learning the village way
   of weeding, hoeing dirt
   with a snub blade, hauling
branches on backs
   in this little African glimpse,
Lady of the House, Topista,
   like the Widow's Mite,
   squeezes passion fruit
   into a large jar, doles
two spoonfuls of raw sugar,
   like cloudy crystals, like gold
dust, serves dessert.

Widow's Mite (Mark 12:41-44, Luke 21: 1-4): In this Gospel tale, an impoverished widow donates two small coins in the face of wealthy people who donate much more. Jesus explains that small sacrifices mean more to God than the extravagant donations of the rich who can easily afford it.

Orchestra Concert Walk

We three walk to the middle school as a family. It's only a few long blocks. Eliot (13) slops along in his shoes, one size too big, new. His last pair were two sizes too small. "We should've doubled up your shocks," Lisa says. "Want Papa to carry you?" "Like Yoda and Luke," I say. "No, Papa," Eliot shirks. "We'll walk at your pace," Lisa says. Five minutes more, and we're late. Above and below, the sun dims, twilight, and, like any day, the clouds glow pink and purple and orange, like autumn leaves, burning, turning, flaring before browning, snuffing out. Only a few thin black phone lines cut up our view. I jot a few words in my notebook as we walk:

Thin cirrus
  clouds behind
telephone lines—
dusk in Kansas.

We arrive on time. Our son takes off his socks, rubs his heels, red blisters puffing up.

Flag Scoop

Alice seems to like the clean sewn edge of the red drill team flag, how when the triangle of cloth spun, the material sung, made its own wind. Alice spun the pole that held the flag end over end, as a twirler would, but bigger, like a bow stick working.

Jack McCann conjured up our marching band, complete with drill team, pretty much from nothing, riding into town in his indigo Pinto, wearing a white cowboy hat and flashing his metal teeth, two stepping his roper boot feet to his own cadence, his own tune. He rallied the middle school parents to back him, to buy drums and flags and t-shirts. We marched in denim blues, no time or cash for formal uniforms yet, but we had spirit, and McCann had us play the tunes for each branch of the service as part of our program, ending with "Anchors Aweigh."

Alice is my sister, and I can tell she loves the snap of the flag, the dance to the snare and bass drum beat. She's my little sister, a sevie, seventh grader, and she's danced since she can walk. I march behind her and the other young ones, girls with red scarves tied to their arms, since we don't yet have uniforms for dance, and my sister beams, her teeth slicked with Vaseline to make them pop and sparkle.

My drum in its harness is a little heavy. The carrier is a cast-off, the heaviest model. I'm on the biggest bass drum, swinging my big mallets like a gorilla, the heads of the mallets big and thick and almost square, like swinging sledge hammers. The mallets are also cast-off, old models from Northside, which has the cash to cast away all that's old and lost.

This is our first parade, and, a late entry, we're placed almost last, marching behind a troupe of horsemen on big brown stallions. Their tails wave at flies, whip and swish, big black flyswatters, and we must watch their rumps the whole walk, as they trot to catch up, their feet blurring and wobbling; as they slow and stutter step; as they spook and jot at a diagonal and are righted by their riders, the horses' eyes, like pirate eyes, behind black blinders. The riders wear greys and blues with funny box caps, like nurses wear. They're Civil War re-enactors, complete with brown rifles with brassy bolts and actions.

When they stop, they poop. The horses drop big brown pies into the street that the flies light to. The poop is a ripple, with a big fat base winding to the top, which sometimes comes to a folded-over tip, as with an ice cream cone poured from a machine, the top like the droopy tip and top of a dwarf cap.

Alice and her peers march on through, trying to side step poop, swinging their flags like blenders, like pinwheels, like swords, and Alice catches the edge of one of those horse pies on accident, and poop holds to the red fabric and is flung, spots of poop like dirt clods up and into the air and into the crowd. Poo on faces, on arms, on legs. There is a cry. And there is wiping with whatever is present—a blanket, a t-shirt. The curses come, but we march on. It is our job to keep going, no matter what. And we do, Alice's flag flinging just droplets of poo now, like a gentle rain, like the last cycle on the car wash machine.

Snatching Rip's Hi-Hat

Maria (Helen of the four-high school area) belongs to Rip, a drummer/body builder, a senior at North. He's built like He-Man or Stretch Armstrong. You could pull, and he'd be all muscle, plastic, pink. No fat. Rip is ripped, though we don't call it that in 1992.

It's jazz cabaret season, and we kids travel from school to school with our horns and drums in hard black cases, one busful, and play while our parents slurp store-bought sauce and spaghetti, fund raisers to buy more trumpets and saxes and drums.

When we unpack the back of the bus, we discover our hi-hat's missing, probably left in the band room, and everyone knows you need that hi-hat swish, swish, da-swish for big band. North is Rip's school, and so his set's up front, an all-burgundy maple drumset with Zildjian A's and Z's. Top notch. Everyone knows you don't borrow or lend cymbals or drums. They get bent or dented or walk off.

We play first, in three minutes, and so we need to find a hi-hat fast. Deandre sits cool by the black and yellow Shawnee Mission West drum set slouched like he's sipping from a cigarette. I ask, and he says, "No, fool." McFee sits atop the East white-and-blue rhythm ship. He tightens the knot of his tie, says, "Too rich for you."

One minute left, and I don't see Rip, but see beautiful Maria in his spot, her silhouette like a glimpse caught from a doll house window, her hair dark like the Missouri River, her eyes like those winks of light distant planes flash at night, part star, part mechanical, metaphysical magic. (You see me? You see?)

Rip's hi-hat is all modern, a dry cymbal on bottom, a bright one on top, something popular for those with the cash. I reach for the hi-hat neck, just beneath the cymbals, clamped shut, and pick the heavy metal bugger up with a swoop and lug it over to our school's set.

We're on. I open the hat halfway and give it a funky swish and click, my drumstick like a twirler's baton or conductor's wand, one motion, and the rest's magic, music. Our band leader stands and waves his little T-Rex arms, a little too close to his body: "Uh-1, Uh-2, Uh-1-2-3-4." I swing hard as I can, hit through the ride cymbal with each stroke, attack and ring, chick the hi-hat hard on 2 & 4. Like steering a big dump truck, I drive the big band, lay down time like thick tire tracks. (Follow, follow).

About quarter-way into the tune, Rip enters the room, a thick shadow in the indigo cabaret. He stoops and looks. "Yep, that's my hat." He stops. Is that a grin? He swings an arm around Maria and sits and watches, like a man watches a cock fight, waiting, waiting for the blood. I try not to look. When we finish, Rip stands and flexes and claps, his biceps bulge like big tree knots, jut through his white dress shirt. He flashes his perfect teeth, dons his black sports jacket, and comes to the stand. Is North next? I thought West was? Rip just stands in front of me, buff, mountain-like, then holds out his ham-hand, and we shake, more like he crushes me, my fingers in a clamp, a winch, not malicious, though; this is his regular grip.

"Nice one, mighty flea," he says, and I clamp shut the shiny hat and hand him the stand, my arm trembling. He takes his hi-hat back, like whisking a broom away by the handle, nothing for him, and as he passes, I look, and Maria's winking, wagging a finger at me. Her pleas must've saved me again.

Speakeasy Gig, or Playing for Me

Our town, town of William Allen White, decides to host a speakeasy, a four-stop tour of drinks and eats, and I'm asked to read some jazz poetry in the basement of the *Gazette*, a dusty, dirty bin for yellowed papers and seized-up printing machines, toppled boxes of moveable type. The singer I'm paired with spills her drink on her purple velvet flapper dress, her gin and tonic a comet, a crater splash on the floor. She starts to wipe the mess with a towel, and I say, "Don't worry. No one will notice," and she laughs and stands and says, "But my dress!" "Can't tell with that either," and she says, "Thank goodness for velvet," "And dark speakeasies," I say, and I re-string her mic cord so she won't trip, and she says, "Thanks, sweets, but I won't be dancing tonight," though she does jitter her shoulders like a flapper when she sings the Amy Winehouse throw-back, and she turns, spots I've been watching, and says, "And let's give a hand for that jazz poet _____," and they clap, though I know they'd rather just jitterbug and foxtrot and Charleston to her and her laptop hooked to my amp, her and her electric band. "I only have 15 minutes of jazz," she says she said when they asked her to sing tonight. I do seven minutes of poems, do kicks on cymbal and snare drum, standing, solo swiftly, and am done. She says she's back from New York, singing and modeling, shots and spots, and we're stuck in this corner in the dark in an unpaid benefit gig for the rich, know there's no lower, and when the barman sees me setting levels, turning knobs, stringing cable and running cords before, snapping three prong and two prong adaptors for her, he says, "Oh, I thought you two were a couple," and I say, "No, musicians just know how to comp for each other," and she winks and hands me a free CD, and I hand her my book, and I know we won't kiss, but she asks me to pose for a shot with her phone, and says, "In this one, act like you're playing for me."

2. (MORE) NEW MUSIC OR BOSSA NOVA, THAT NEW NEW THING

Dennis Chambers, Recorded

What I wanted
   was a minute or two
of his groove, up close
   caught on tape
along with filtered through
   my own two ears,
so I snuck a pocket recorder in
   to the Dennis Chambers clinic,
sat up front at the foot
   of his bass drum,
tangled in silver
   cymbal sands, like a man
in a thicket. Somehow,
   I pressed the play button,
and out came my baby sister's
   voice, and Chambers heard, miffed,
and hit harder, and knocked a cymbal
   down beside me, felled it
with one stroke, and that
   sent me packing, recorder
shut off, head down,
   ears aslant.

Bossa Nova, That New Thing

I show up at Shawnee Mission West
   for this high school jam,
and someone calls
   "Girl from Ipanema,"
and I'm lost.
   I've never played bossa
or samba, and I don't
   know the first thing,
and so a kindly teacher
   shows me how
to cross-stick click
   across drum-
rim, but I don't
   get the rhythm,
can't think, can't feel
   just what he means,
and so I'm sent to Doug,
   drummer for Sons
of Brasil, who,
   after my audition,
takes me
   on a tour
of the rhythms
   of Brazil, a history
in the hands
   and feet, the heart
like a surdo,
   Brazilian bass drum,
thumping, 1
   +3, +1, +3,
come on, come
   with me.

Blues Guitar

I teach Ian
  a train beat
on brushes, the grey wire
  whisks huffing
the drum head—
  1e+A2e+A—
so he can switch
  rhythms with James,
who's learned some
  Cash on guitar,
"Folsom Prison Blues,"
  James—who goes all dark
  like a lightbulb wire
that goes bright orange
  then flashes out,
when his father dies, who
  takes up blues guitar,
acoustic, just his fingers
  and string, just
hum of hollow guitar,
  then that moan,
his voice low low for 13.
  James doesn't last
the year.

How James Keller Lost His Groove

We get done with the set, and the house music clicks on, and the tune's groovin', and I take a few steps from behind the (drum)set, dance, and one of the new guys says, "Yeah, man. Get it! Move," and I grow all self-conscious, and stop, and he says, "Come on, man. Dance! I saw you do it," and I'm this little white guy from the burbs, and these new jazzers are older and black, and I don't have it, have lost my groove to dance, can't, and next gig I'm not asked back.

One Week Off

Richard Hoss takes the stage,
   large in his gold and coal African shirt, sings,
he always sings, and everyone asks him to—
   —sit in, to stand and raise his colossal
bullfrog voice to the rafters, the ceiling, the club
   top. Hoss was once a drummer,
fought over dues, gave notice of a week off
   after 12 years on, and was fired. I've seen
his union papers. All he always wanted
   was one week off with his son.

Mix'n'

Some white guys sit in at the black jam at the KC Chez Paree ("Home Place"), 18th and Vine, January, 1946, and the police break up the show/moment, haul those white boys out, and the board of police say the officers were "acting correctly in stopping the weekly interracial jazz concerts as 'dancing, hot music, and possible liquor' spelled a potential disturbance," while "Carl Johnson, NAACP head, . . . held that refusal by police to sell tickets to white patrons was a civil liberties violation," and up-city in Westport, Bird, on a quick stop off the road from the coast, smokes a joint with some chalk-colored boys in a painter's apartment after his gig. Hands to horn, he don't mind mixin'. We all have something we can teach.

quoted passage, "Jim Crow in KC," DOWNBEAT, April 1946

"Seven Days"

Colaiuta, who
   can play as well
in 5 or 7
   as in 4, who
hits his little splash cymbals
   like skipping rocks
each hit: a skip, how
Colaiuta can make
   Sting's "Seven Days"
pop song sound
   as if playing
 in 5 is a child's game,
   double dutch
rope hop.

Weekend Gig

We come to the roundabouts
   at the edge of town—
Highway 50 to central Kansas,
   the turnpike (I-335) to Lawrence.
We're headed to the blue dot,
trunk loaded full of drums,
   a brushes gig—
snare drum and cajón. Inside,
our suitcases stacked next to our son.
   We'll crash at my parents'
when the gig's done.
We've been at it 12 years now,
   once a month, the music—
a breath, a drug, the only kind
   of party I've ever
loved, been any good at, done.

**Commencement Processional:
"Triumphant March" from "Aida"**

for Gary Ziek

Gary holds up a fist,
   last time through
this tune; his trumpet up,
   his fingers pump
three keys; bell of his horn
   catches blonde hardwood light—
everything stops, everything starts
   when we rise and cross
this stage.

New Tune, Juan's Song

Ellington's ink is still wet,
   black dots across
5 lines, across white,
   when he asks me
to copy all the parts.
   show tonight at 5.

*Along with playing trombone, Juan Tizol also composed and served as musical score copier for the Duke Ellington band.

New Tune

One plucked note, then two strummed,
   Lisa makes her slow way through
a new tune. Notes first; words later.
   I listen to her hum.

Middle School Drummer

Talley: I know you're grown, but I always remember you as my little middle school drummer, always just right, played just what we needed, right there with us. Comes from listening.

3. ELECTION DAY

The Donald

He's the kind of guy, like Henry VIII,
   you try to hide your women from,
to whom you might bow as he goes by,
   but would spit at or pick a fight with
if he weren't richer, who swoops away
   in his black Armani and Rolls, who bites
each coin and riffles each fat-banded cash stack
   like Uncle Scrooge McDuck, swimming
in lucre, in gold wave troughs and crests.

[Hillary's sunk]

Hillary's sunk
  because of her
emails, but Trump
  just can't
stop Tweeting.
  While she
covers up,
  he just can't stop
showing himself—
  a boy at the beach
toddling, enamored
  with his own
small parts.

for Michael Smith

Golden Shower

The firework sparks
   arc
in a shower, yellow-gold:
can't call it just what
   I want
in this age of Trump.

Patsy

That morning, when the senate gavel
comes down, wood on wood,
the sanded clap to order, the call,
Patsy's not there, she
who's always early, always there,
she who rode a Sinclair dinosaur
from Hutch into the statehouse,
her float with the slogan,
"Make the Brownback agenda extinct,"
she who cast one of 88 votes
to override the governor's income tax veto,
and won, celebrated with the post,
"You're waking up in a Kansas
where the Brownback experiment
has ended. Good morning."
But Patsy did not
make it long
into that new dawn.
As with the old, who make it
through winter, only to pass
at the first of spring,
so, too, with Patsy. Her voice,
her vote lasts, though,
like so many careful words
placed on a page.

*Patsy Terrell's Hutchinson parade float featured her attached with reins to a Sinclair brontosaurus painted white and dressed in Democrat blue. Patsy was a writer and marketing consultant before turning to Kansas politics. She was 55.

We Read (#2)

One day in, and I will read
protest poems at the coffee shop
tonight in blue dot Lawrence.
Will the bean grinder rat-a-tat clap
when I stand and read,
mic to mouth, my voice
loud, but trembling,
in air?

21 Jan. 2017, Kansas

Election Day Map

We're not purple,
 but at least
we're pink.

Wednesday, 9 Nov. 2016

4. MEN & WOMEN

Change Drawer Lip Balm

My truck's
   headliner's come undone,
ripples in road wind
when I go to pick Lisa up.
First date. She says
she likes a man
who keeps lip balm
in his truck change drawer.

Good Form

In *Good Man*, O'Connor's
   old woman
is told by her killer,
  if you'd have had a gun
to your head every minute,
  you'd have been golden,
and I know, as I lift
   beside two beauties
in pink Spandex and yoga pants,
   my form best it's ever been,
for me the same is true.

Eclipse

My wife and I
  look up
at the sun,
  cardboard glasses on
with their thick silver lenses,
though we don't
  hold hands,
we should, though
  the sun's there,
it's also gone,
  covered, snuffed, black-
ened for a breath, stunned.

Crickets begin.

Emporia, KS, 21 Aug. 2017, 1:06 pm

Pit Stop

Sunset, and L cracks
   the car windows,
and I pump the gas.

Not long, and we're back
   on the road, sunlight
our guide.

Out Again

"You don't want to know
   what she said,"
Chud tells me, after he'd seen
   my ex-wife
at a party in KC, a hip
   loft party, a place
I'd never be. A tomato
   hits the window
of the coffee shop,
   when I'm out
with a new girl. My wife
   was like that.

Because I'm Already Involved

Amber wanted a $300 bottle
of Creed perfume, told
everyone on Facebook. I once
dated Amber, so I send her
a $15 sample, the size
of a cigarette. At least
I can do something, send
some scent, if even
a pinch.

We see what we want

The woman at the table
  by the window
could be my ex-wife,
  pregnant, with two older girls,
gossiping, a little chubby,
  but glowing, nectarine-cheeked,
éclair rich and sophisticate,
  a little lumpy. I love her still.

Pear Shaped

(Man and Woman prepare for an exercise class at the gym. They set up their steps, place their towels and cell phones and water bottles and hand weights.)

Man (talking to someone, unseen): They look pear shaped, and I love pears.

Woman: What'd you say?

Man: They look pear shaped, and I love pears.

Woman: Oh. I thought you said, "*You* look pear shaped, and I love pears."

Man: No. Heh. Perhaps that, too.

Woman: Really. (She stretches.)

Man: I hadn't thought of that, but I do like you.

Woman: Like how I look?

Man: Sure. That, too?

Woman: You're not too bad lookin' either.

Man: Thanks. I try. It's why I'm here.

Woman: That and to look at cute girls?

Man: Frosting.

Woman: Me, too. The guys that come to this class are usually cute. Too few, but cupcake cute.

Man: *Butt* cupcake cute?

Woman: Sure, sweets.

(She pats him on the butt.)

5. KIDS

HiFi

In our mall,
   they play country.
When little,
   our son said,
"There's people singin'
   in them holes,"
his finger
pointed to the speaker,
   his ear
to the air.

T. Rex, Sternberg Museum, Hays, KS

The big plastic jaws
   yawn, enlarge, and the body
moves in with a roar.

A toddler runs,
   and his father grins
and lends a hand, a thumb.

Day Off

I.
The machine sputters,
   when I get E and I water
from the soda rack, and we sit
   in the a/c
and eat sandwiches
   on our day off.

I decorate
   a sandwich bag
with "peace, love, & freedom,"
   drawing a peace sign,
heart, and flag. Wonder
   if they'll hang that up?

II.
L gets her hair done.
I go buy us some liquid soap.
E wants to wait in the car,
but I make him go in.

The Fourth

Outside, the streets are on fire, and boys stand by garage doors with ball caps flipped back, lit sticks in their hands, punk cherries waiting to kiss fuses, start it, light it, light it all up again.

Afterburner at the Up-Down Retro Video Game Café

I can still dodge & spin
   on *Afterburner* (again),
& Don sings that Top Gun ("Danger Zone") song,
while I refuel in the air, jet
   past stage one, go slow & strafe
a line of grounded planes, then learn how to lock on
   with missiles again.

Cute Li'l Groot,
   toddler tree,
he dances, and we forget
   the teeth and claws,
the explosions around.
   So it is with kids.
Nothing we do
   calls as loud
as that inner rhythm,
   the pound of that
fast, spangled soundtrack.

Neighborhood Hood

Like being held
  in Vader's choke hold,
Derrek's got me held
  by the neck
in his brown leather gloves,
  lifted above the steps
until I kick him
  in the nuts
and am let go.

6. DOCUMENTARY SHOTS

Wedding Shots

The paid wedding photographer
   tells me to back off,
though I'm shooting from just around
   a column and am in none of her shots
and am not sidling, elbow to elbow, with her,
but am way out of the way;
she's had to go out of hers
   to even be here, in my spot,
at least a stone's throw, and I tell her
my trip to NYC was paid for
   so I could come and shoot,
uncle to the groom.

Your Portrait

It used to be the very rich
  would have to dress up
in their finest threads
  and sit real still,
while a hired painter
  sketches, then brushes
their faces and fancy clothes
  onto canvas.
But now any ole Jane or Jim
  can slap on some nice clothes
and step into the bathroom
  with their phone,
and snap the same thing—
from painting sitting
  to selfie.

Photos in the Field
   Bertha Keller Rabas (64), Gary Rabas (46)

And that visit, your mother
   and you
walked out into the wheat, green,
   gangly, youthful, so we
could snap pictures
   of what you are, were,
tenders of the wheat.

Saving

There's an ATM
   in the Taco Bell
      parking lot—
and I go there a lot,
   put cash in, save
for the storm

that fills my basement,
   so I can
get the water out,
   put a skirt of concrete
'round my house,
   angled down,
angled out.

Water Break

Lisa makes a Walmart run, gets
   a case of bottled water. This morning,
when we turned the faucet knobs,
   a hissing sound, and nothing, not a drop.

*water main break, city of 25,000 without water, Thursday 20 July 2017, Emporia, KS

Fuzzy's

At Fuzzy's in Manhattan. When they first opened, owned and run by two frat boys, they called the place The Pink Taco, and I wrote protest postcards under pseudonyms (James Xavier III, Hansel Pomeroy), saying that name's crude; you'll be no favorite with the ladies.

Don't Look

So many men
   spit, when they piss,
loogie into the trough
   to loosen up, look
down, look up, but
   never over and out
at you.

Lisa Redoes the Room

After all of that measuring, the long yellow metal tape
   with its square silver reel, the hammer's finality,
the tiny tack nail sinks into the newly painted wall.

7. ECLIPSE

Eclipse, Emporia, Kansas

That dim, like
  the green
before thunderstorm,
  but orange.
You
  look up.

Transitory

How the breath
 comes and goes—
the flame's flicker,
 the ocean foam,
the twigs
 in the wren nest.

Cottonwood

Half the leaves
   in sun, half
in shadow. One hundred degrees,
   & all I can think of
are the green things, whether
   they're getting enough
water.

The slow turn
of the wind turbines, grey giants
near Salina, blades
like propellers, idling,
pulled by Kansas wind;
the breath of God
comes in a cloud; an open
mouth whistles
over and past tall grasses,
from dust, remakes the world.

Roadtrip, Rainbow

I.
What ancient plainsfolk
must've thought, walking
through tan grass
when they saw a giant rainbow
in the distance, reaching, touching
nothing, before we knew
   the science.

II.
We stop in our van
   on the way to Wichita,
along the flat gray breakdown lane,
the yellow-tan plains,
like low-tide waves,
   and out come the phones
and the snap of photos. How bright
the leg of the arch
near the ground,
   like gold
spilling into grass.

White Hair

My goatee grows white, blanches,
   starting at the tip,
at the paint brush tongue.
   My mother and father live to see it—
my father's hair and beard, snow, ice white,
   my mother's hair, dyed.
Each time I see them I wonder,
   How long?

Write Right Like Buddha-Calm CP

If you can,
   sit up straight
while you write.
   Look at how little
motion Charlie Parker wastes,
body neutral, placid, finger-
tips buzzing above the buttons
   of his whole horn.

CP: Charlie Parker

Weed Whip Line, Caught

After I mow,
   I weed whip
the little hickory starts,
   sometimes tangling
and wrapping the line 'round
   the thicker, pencil-thick shoots,
jumbling everything,
   like cat's cradle, like
caught floss, like
   kite string
in a taller tree.

Friday, 5 O'Clock

That weightlessness
   at 10 till 5, the clock now
like birdsong or frogsong, background—
   no longer
the marching boot stomps
   to work to,
eat to, piss to.

Strings

How you force a smile,
    a laugh with your boss, how
like a ventriloquist's dummy
    or Geppetto's puppet,
you are taut, pulled
    upright by too too many
strings.

Line

My actor calls "line" five times
   in two minutes, can't remember
what I've written, curtain
   in about an hour. Could I, should I
act in this one myself?

Brown Suede Sports Coat

When I went back
   to jazz,
my mother got me a
   brown suede sports coat.
I wore it to almost every gig.
   "How come
I don't have one of those
   snazzy coats?" Biff said.
"Luck," I said,
   head injured,
divorced, living
   back at home.

Wait in the Lot

Sometimes, you go in
   and look at rope
   in the hardware store.
Others, you wait
   in the car, stare past
the sinking winter sun.

Poet

As with the crossword
   or jumble, I play
at words
   each day.

ABOUT THE AUTHOR

Poet Laureate of Kansas (2017-2019), Kevin Rabas teaches at Emporia State University, where he leads the poetry and playwriting tracks and chairs the Department of English, Modern Languages, and Journalism. He has nine other books, including *Lisa's Flying Electric Piano*, a Kansas Notable Book and Nelson Poetry Book Award winner. Rabas's plays have been produced across Kansas and in North Carolina and San Diego, and his work has been nominated for the Pushcart Prize six times. He is the recipient of the Emporia State President's Award for Research and Creativity and is the winner of the Langston Hughes Award for Poetry, the Victor Contoski Poetry Award, the Jerome Johanning Playwriting Award, and the Salina New Voice Award.

PRIMARY CURRENT INFLUENCES

Literary: Kevin Young (*Book of Hours*), Terrance Hayes, Denise Duhamel, Aimee Nezhukumatathil (*Lucky Fish*), Ted Kooser, Tim Seibles, Naomi Shihab Nye, William Stafford, Yusef Komunyakaa, Kim Addonizio (*Tell Me, Mortal Trash*), Dorianne Laux, Langston Hughes, Michael Ondaatje, Claudia Rankine (*Citizen*), Ntozake Shange, Michael S. Harper, Thomas Lux, Tracy Letts (*August: Osage County; Superior Donuts*), David Auburn (*Proof*), Scott Cairns (*The Theology of Doubt*), Ta-Nehisi Coates, Fred Moten, Tyehimba Jess (*Olio*), Traci Brimhall.

Musical: Charlie Parker; Sting ("Seven Days"); Keith Jarrett Trio ("U Dance"); DeJohnette, Grenadier, Medeski, & Scofield (*Hudson*); Matthew Brewer (*Solo Conception*); Madeleine Peyroux

("Blue Alert" -- Leonard Cohen, lyrics; Anjani Thomas, music); Mark Lowrey (*Live at Jardine's*); Taylor Swift (*1989*); Ryan Adams (*1989*); Jason Isbell; Josh Ritter; Dollar Brand/Abdullah Ibrahim (*South Africa, Zimbabwe*); Miles Davis (*Kind of Blue*); John Coltrane (*Coltrane's Sound*).

ACKNOWLEDGMENTS

The author gratefully acknowledges the editors of the following publications, in which versions of the following poems first appeared:

"Not Done" in *Rock and Sling*

"New Tune, Juan's Song," "Middle School Drummer," "We Read (#2)," and "[Hillary's Sunk]" in *Poetrybay*

WORDS OF THANKS

I am blessed to have a family that appreciates and encourages my writing, including Lisa, Eliot, Joyce, Gary, and Alicia. Thanks also go to my writer and artist friends, as well as supporters, who offered encouragement, including Dennis Etzel Jr, Laura Cossey, Val Bontrager, Randy and Amy Carlson, Joyce and Gary Rabas, Alicia and Sam Styles, Selah Saterstrom, Denise Low, Dan Jaffe, Artt Frank, Jen Rae Hartman, Cary Strong, Jen McConnell Doron, Thomas and Carol Ferrel, Stacey Eisele, Max McCoy, Elizabeth Dodd, Jeb and Stuart Rosebrook, Tyler Sheldon, Alex Arceneaux, Joseph DeLuca, Jason Ryberg, Will Leathem, Marina Jaffe, Amy Sage Webb, Bill Sheldon, William Clamurro, Masami Sugimori, Ramona Vreeland, Traci Brimhall, Kevin Willmott, William J. Harris, Beth Moritz and Leonard Brauner, Ruth Moritz, Paula and Rick Keltner, Leslie VonHolten, Julie Mulvihill, Paula Sauder, Kevin Kienholz, Rachelle Smith, Kat O'Meara, Steve Catt, Mel Storm, Jim and Anna Ryan, Glenn North, and Lisa Moritz.

Thanks to Michael Pelletier for his invaluable help curating, organizing, and editing this manuscript.

Thanks to Caryn Mirriam-Goldberg and Mike Graves for the blurbs.

Many thanks also go to my editor and publisher, Tracy Million Simmons.

WWW.MEADOWLARK-BOOKS.COM

Specializing in Books by Authors from the Heartland since 2014

meadowlark-books.com

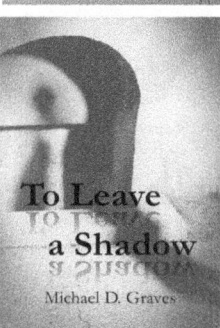
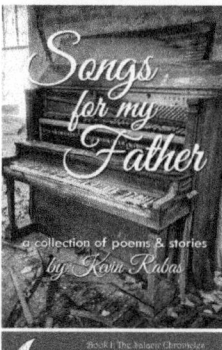

www.ingramcontent.com/pod-product-compliance
Lightning Source LLC
Chambersburg PA
CBHW051659040426
42446CB00009B/1209